debbie macomber

Popular author Debbie Macomber has discovered that women's fiction and knitting go together like a hand and glove — a knit glove, of course.

In her books *The Shop on Blossom Street* and *A Good Yarn*, Debbie introduces us to two groups of women from highly diverse backgrounds. The women join knitting classes at a small yarn shop in Seattle and soon discover that friendship truly knows no boundaries.

With more than 60 million copies of her books in print and an ever-growing base of fans who eagerly await the release of each new novel, you might think that Debbie is simply too busy to do anything but write. However, Debbie is herself an avid knitter who believes strongly in "giving back" to her community. One way she accomplishes this is by drawing attention to worthy causes through her books.

It was while working on *The Shop on Blossom Street* that Debbie learned about an organization called Warm Up America! Knitters and crocheters create 7" x 9" blocks for this charity group. The blocks are joined into blankets and donated to the needy. Debbie became one of the first board members for Warm Up America!, and she continues to work tirelessly on its behalf.

In fact, Debbie is delighted to let you know that all her profits from the sales of both *Knit Along with Debbie Macomber* pattern books — *The Shop on Blossom Street* and *A Good Yarn* — will be donated to Warm Up America! to support their work in communities across the United States. She urges everyone who uses these patterns to take a few minutes to knit or crochet a block for this worthy cause. On page 43, you will find out how, with just a little bit of yarn, you can make a real difference.

Debbie also hopes that **this collection of twelve stylish knit fashions** will inspire you to discover the rich rewards of knitting for yourself and those you love.

LEISURE ARTS, INC.
Little Rock, Arkansas

a word from LEISURE ARTS and MIRA books

Read The Books That Inspired the Projects

Debbie Macomber's fan-favorite novel, *The Shop on Blossom Street*, introduced us to four fascinating women who share their joys and heartaches while learning to knit in a Seattle yarn shop. This best-selling story is now joined by Debbie's next book in the fiction series: *A Good Yarn* — and what a good yarn it is! Three women of varying ages learn the art of knitting in this delightful tale of love and unexpected friendship.

And now you can experience the rewards of knitting, just like the women of Blossom Street! Leisure Arts is pleased to offer two knitting instruction books as companions to the novels.

Knit Along with Debbie Macomber — The Shop on Blossom Street features instructions for 11 darling baby blankets. The second knitting book, *Knit Along with Debbie Macomber— A Good Yarn*, contains 12 patterns for beautiful hats, socks, sweaters, a poncho, and more.

Laced with excerpts from the novels, each knitting instruction book retains the warm, friendly atmosphere created by this gifted author. Read Debbie Macomber's insightful stories of love, then knit up a little creativity from Leisure Arts.

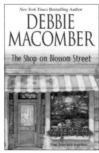
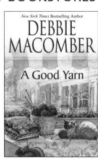

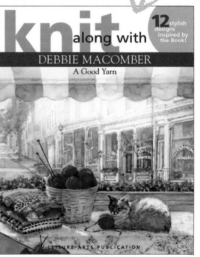

meet the women

from *A Good Yarn*

LYDIA HOFFMAN

Knitting saved my life. It saw me through two lengthy bouts of cancer.

I'd just turned sixteen the first time I was diagnosed, and I learned to knit while undergoing chemotherapy. The chemo was dreadful, but because of knitting, I was able to endure those endless hours of weakness and severe nausea. With two needles and a skein of yarn, I felt I could face whatever I had to. By the time I was officially in remission, I knew I had to make a choice about what I should do with the rest of my life. I, Lydia Anne Hoffman, resolved to make my mark on the world. In retrospect, that sounds rather melodramatic, but a year ago it was exactly how I felt.

*What, you might ask, did I do that was so life-changing and profound? I opened a yarn store on Blossom Street in Seattle. I had an inheritance from my grandparents and gambled every cent on starting my own business. Me, who knew nothing about finances, profit-and-loss statements or business plans. I sank every dime I had in the world into what I **did** know, and that was yarn and knitters. I always say that A Good Yarn is my affirmation of life.*

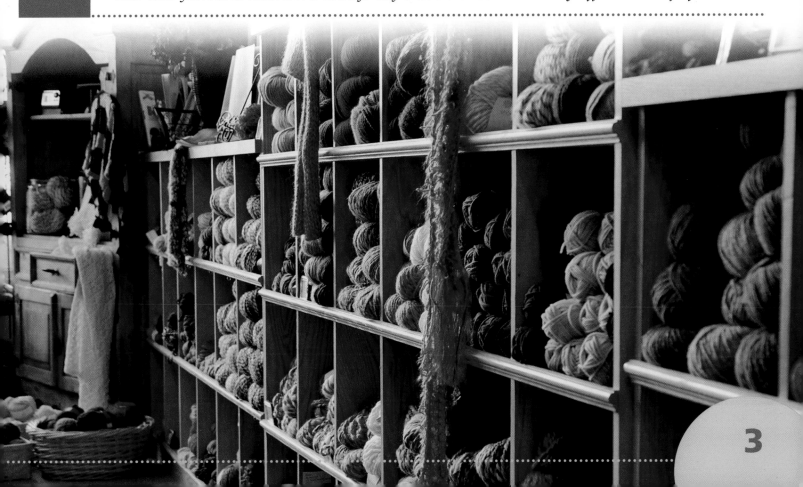

Elise Beaumont had scrimped and saved, wanting to build her own home on her own small piece of land. After months of visiting housing developments, she put down a large chunk of cash. She'd assumed the developer was a reputable one; to put it bluntly, he wasn't. The company filed bankruptcy within a month. Now, she had no savings and mounting legal bills.

After a visit to her attorney's office, Elise walked down Blossom Street. In the window of A Good Yarn, she saw a sign that advertised knitting classes. She might not be able to enjoy her retirement the way that she'd hoped, but she thought knitting might keep her mind off her financial difficulties.

Elise opened the door and a small bell rang.

"Good morning," a pleasant-faced woman greeted her.

"Yes, it is," Elise said, instantly warmed by the younger woman's friendliness. "I've come to inquire about classes," she said. "I recently retired and thought I'd take up knitting again."

"Would you like to sign up for the sock class? I'm sure you'd enjoy it."

"Yes, I think I would." Elise opened her purse. "How many will be in the class?" she asked as she signed the check.

"I'd like to limit it to six. You're the first person to sign up."

"The first," Elise repeated, and for reasons she could only guess at, being first gave her a sense of pleasure.

"I'm home," Bethanne Hamlin called out as she opened the front door, doing her best to sound cheerful. "Andrew? Annie?"

If not for her children, Bethanne didn't know what she would've done. It was now six months after the divorce had been finalized, and the fog was only starting to clear.

"How'd it go at the employment agency?" her sixteen-year-old daughter asked.

Bethanne sighed. "Not good." After all these years outside the job market, Bethanne didn't think she possessed any saleable skills. "I was thinking of selling cosmetics," she said tentatively.

"Mom! You're great at lots of things, but you'd make a terrible salesperson. You should do something just for you," Annie insisted. "I'm not even talking about a job. Isn't there anything you'd like to do just for fun?"

"I saw a yarn store on Blossom Street the other day. I used to enjoy knitting."

"You can do it," Annie told her firmly. "You're not putting this off the way you have everything else." She pulled out the Yellow Pages, scooped up the phone and punched the number before Bethanne could protest. Half a minute later, Annie replaced the portable phone. "You'll be learning to knit socks. You're going, Mom, and I won't take no for an answer."

Apparently their roles had reversed, although this was news to Bethanne. It must've happened while she wasn't paying attention.

In Courtney's opinion, this entire plan of her father's was unfair. Her senior year of high school would be spent with her Grandma Pulanski in Seattle. While the kids she'd grown up with graduated together, she'd be stuck halfway across the country. There was no other place for Courtney to go while her father was working in Brazil. She'd been with her grandmother now for exactly a week.

"Courtney?" Vera Pulanski yelled from the bottom of the stairs. "I need to run a few errands. I want you to come with me."

Their first stop was the library. They drove to the grocery store next. Courtney must have been introduced to thirty people and not a single one was under seventy.

"Now Blossom Street," her grandmother said.

At the yarn shop, Courtney wandered through the store. A display scarf knitted in variegated colors was gorgeous, and there was a felted hat and purse, a vest and a sweater. Five minutes later, Vera placed her purchases by the cash register. Courtney hurried over.

"Did you see the socks?" her grandmother asked.

Courtney nodded. "Those new yarns are really amazing, aren't they?"

"Sign her up." Her grandmother told the shop owner.

"Sign me up for what?" Courtney wanted to know.

"The sock class," her grandmother explained. "It's time you met people and got involved."

Courtney smiled, trying to show she was grateful. She just hoped at least one other person in the sock class was under ninety years old.

lydia's socks

Lydia chose this design for her sock class. The self-patterning yarn created the intricate appearance of these socks entirely on its own.

▰▰▰▱ INTERMEDIATE

Lydia's Tip: This is a basic sock pattern. Once you understand the construction, you can make changes as you desire. The Cuff can be worked in K2, P2 ribbing and the different sections can be knit with different colors.

Size	Finish Foot Circumference
Small	7¹/₂" (19 cm)
Medium	8" (20.5 cm)
Large	8¹/₂" (21.5 cm)

Size Note: Instructions are written for size Small, with sizes Medium and Large in braces { }. Instructions will be easier to read if you circle all the numbers pertaining to your size. If only one number is given, it applies to all sizes.

MATERIALS

Light Weight Self Striping Yarn:
[1.76 ounces, 152 yards, 50 grams, 140 meters per skein]: 2{2-3} skeins
Two 16" (40.5 cm) or 24" (61 cm) Circular knitting needles each, sizes 2 (2.75 mm) **and** 3 (3.25 mm) **or** sizes needed for gauge
Tapestry needle

GAUGE: With **smaller** size needle, in Stockinette Stitch, 24 sts and 36 rnds = 4" (10 cm)

KNITTING IN THE ROUND WITH TWO CIRCULAR NEEDLES

This method is an alternative to working with the stitches divided on three or four double pointed needles. Instead, the stitches are divided on only two circular needles. Each needle is used independently of the other. While you are knitting across the first half of stitches with the other end of the same needle, the second needle will hang out of the way, with the stitches at the center of the cable. Then you will pick up both ends of the second needle, and work across it while the first needle hangs.

CUFF

With larger size needle, cast on 44{48-52} sts on one circular needle.

Slip the last 22{24-26} sts cast on onto the second circular needle, placing them at the center of the cable.

Push the sts on the first needle to the tip at the other end *(Fig. A)*. Place a marker in any st to mark first needle.

Fig. A

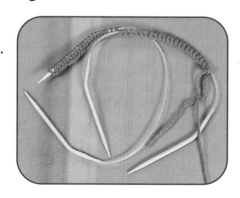

Instructions continued on page 8.

*S*ome of the new yarns were designed to create an intricate pattern when knitted. I found it amazing to view a finished pair of socks, knowing the design had been formed by the yarn itself and not the knitter.

—Lydia

Move the first needle so that it is in front of and parallel to the cable of the second needle (*Fig. B*). Holding both needles in your left hand, straighten your stitches so that they're not twisted around the needles.

Fig. B

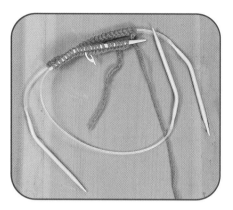

When going from one needle to the next, keep the yarn between the first and last stitches snug to prevent a hole.

Using the other end of the same needle, work in K1, P1 ribbing across the first needle.

Slide the stitches to the center of the cable and turn your work. Slide the stitches that are on the second needle from the cable to the point and continue working in K1, P1 ribbing.

Continue to work in K1, P1 ribbing in the same manner until ribbing measures approximately 2" (5 cm) from cast on edge.

LEG
Knit each round until piece measures approximately 3$\frac{1}{4}${3$\frac{1}{2}$-3$\frac{3}{4}$}"/8.5{9-9.5} cm from cast on edge.

Changing to smaller size needles, knit each round until piece measures approximately 6$\frac{1}{2}${7-7$\frac{1}{2}$}"/16.5{18-19} cm from cast on edge **or** to desired length.

HEEL FLAP
Begin working in rows on the first needle only. The stitches on the second needle won't be used until the Gusset. The following pattern will make the Heel dense and will help prevent it from wearing out.

When instructed to slip a stitch, always slip as if to **purl** with yarn held to **wrong** side.

Row 1: (Slip 1, K1) across.

Row 2: (Slip 1, P1) across.

Repeat Rows 1 and 2 until Heel Flap measures approximately 2$\frac{3}{4}${3-3$\frac{1}{4}$}"/7{7.5-8.5} cm, ending by working Row 2.

TURN HEEL
Begin working in short rows as follows:

Row 1: Slip 1, K 12{14-16}, SSK (*Figs. 5a-c, page 46*), K1, leave remaining 6 sts unworked; turn.

Row 2: Slip 1, P 5{7-9}, P2 tog (*Fig. 8, page 46*), P1, leave remaining 6 sts unworked; turn.

Row 3: Slip 1, K 6{8-10}, SSK, K1; turn.

Row 4: Slip 1, P 7{9-11}, P2 tog, P1; turn.

Rows 5-8: Repeat Rows 3 and 4 twice, adding one st before decrease: 14{16-18} sts.

GUSSET

Begin working with two circular needles in the round.

To pick up and knit stitches, pick up a stitch *(Figs. 11a & b, page 47)* and place it on the left needle, then knit the stitch.

Rnd 1: Still using first needle, knit across the Heel sts, pick up and knit 16{18-20} sts working in end of rows along side of Heel Flap; with the second needle, knit across the Leg; with the first needle, pick up and knit 16{18-20} sts in end of rows along second side of Heel Flap, knit to end of needle: 46{52-58} sts on the first needle and 22{24-26} sts on the second needle.

Rnd 2: With the second needle, knit across; with the first needle, K1, SSK, knit across to last 3 sts, K2 tog *(Fig. 4, page 46)*, K1: 66{74-82} sts.

Rnd 3: Knit around.

Repeat Rnds 2 and 3, 11{13-15} times: 22{24-26} sts on **each** needle.

Work even knitting each round until Foot measures approximately 6½{7½-8}"/16.5{19-20.5} cm from back of Heel or 1¾{2-2}"/4.5{5-5} cm less than total desired Foot length from back of Heel, ending by working across second needle.

TOE

Rnd 1 (Decrease rnd)**:** K1, SSK, knit across first needle to last 3 sts, K2 tog, K1; K1 on second needle, SSK, knit across to last 3 sts, K2 tog, K1: 20{22-24} sts on **each** needle.

Rnd 2: Knit around.

Repeat Rnds 1 and 2, 6{6-7} times: 8{10-10} sts on **each** needle.

GRAFTING

Hold the needles, with one behind the other and **wrong** sides together. Threaded yarn needle should be on right side of work.
Work in the following sequence, pulling yarn through as if to **knit** or as if to **purl** with even tension and keeping yarn under points of needles to avoid tangling and extra loops.

Step 1: Purl first stitch on **front** needle, leave on *(Fig. C)*.

Step 2: Knit first stitch on **back** needle, leave on *(Fig. D)*.

Step 3: Knit first stitch on **front** needle, slip off.

Step 4: Purl next stitch on **front** needle, leave on.

Step 5: Purl first stitch on **back** needle, slip off.

Step 6: Knit next stitch on **back** needle, leave on.

Repeat Steps 3-6 across until all stitches are worked off the needles.

Fig. C

Fig. D

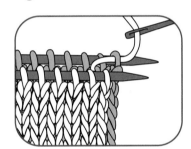

Weave in all yarn ends.

Repeat for second Sock.

Block Socks under a damp towel.

courtney's leg warmers

Once the knitting is done, these leg warmers are made colorful by adding a simple variation of the usual pom-pom. They can be made with just a small amount of yarn leftover from other projects or even with a variegated yarn.

■■□□ **EASY**

Size	Finish Length	Circumference
Child	27" (68.5 cm)	9½" (24 cm)
Adult	32" (81.5 cm)	12" (30.5 cm)

Size Note: Instructions are written for Child's size with Adult's size in braces { }. Instructions will be easier to read if you circle all the numbers pertaining to your size. If only one number is given, it applies to all sizes.

MATERIALS

Fine/Sport Weight Yarn: **FINE 2**
[2½ ounces, 250 yards, 70 grams, 229 meters per skein]: Black – 3{4} skeins
6 colors for pom-poms – 8 yards (7.5 meters) each
Straight knitting needles, sizes 3 (3.25 mm) and 5 (3.75 mm) **or** sizes needed for gauge
Tapestry needle

GAUGE: With larger size needles, in Stockinette Stitch, 24 sts and 32 rows = 4" (10 cm)

UPPER CUFF

With larger size needles and Black, cast on 58{74} sts.

Work in K1, P1 ribbing for 4{6}"/10{15} cm.

BODY

Work in Stockinette Stitch until piece measures approximately 21{24}"/53.5{61} cm from cast on edge, ending by working a **purl** row.

Decrease Row: K2 tog *(Fig. 4, page 46)*, knit across to last 2 sts, K2 tog: 56{72} sts.

Continue to decrease one stitch at each edge, every fourth row, 5 times **more**: 46{62} sts.

Work even for 3 rows.

LOWER CUFF

Change to smaller size needles.

Work in K1, P1 ribbing for 3{5}"/7.5{12.5} cm.

Bind off all stitches in ribbing; cut yarn leaving a long end for sewing.

Repeat for second Leg Warmer.

Instructions continued on page 17.

*The women in my sock class were an interesting mix. I love the way knitting brings people together. As diverse as these women seemed to be, in personality, in background and in age, they were beginning to enjoy each other's company.
—Lydia*

11

fur & bouclé
hat & scarf

With its abundance of color, this hat and scarf set may appear difficult to create, but it isn't! The secret is the combination of variegated yarn and fur-textured yarn. The hat is intended to fit loosely, so don't be alarmed if it seems a little large while you work on it. Another great feature of these boutique-inspired accessories is that they finish up quickly.

■■□□ EASY

Lydia's Tip: When using a textured yarn that easily unravels, it may be helpful to knot the ends. If you'd like your scarf to be wider, use size 13 (9 mm) needles.

MATERIALS
Bulky Weight Textured Yarn: **BULKY 5**
[2½ ounces, 57 yards, 70 grams, 52 meters per skein]: 4 skeins
Bulky Weight Novelty Eyelash Yarn: **BULKY 5**
[1¾ ounces, 60 yards, 50 grams, 54 meters per skein]: 1 skein
Straight knitting needles, size 10½ (6.5 mm)
or size needed for gauge
Yarn needle

GAUGE: In Garter Stitch,
9 sts and 18 rows = 4" (10 cm)

SCARF
Finished Size: 6½" x 54" (16.5 cm x 137 cm)

Holding 2 strands of eyelash yarn together, cast on 15 sts.

Knit 6 rows.

Cut eyelash yarn. Using one strand of textured yarn, knit each row until Scarf measures approximately 52" (132 cm) from cast on edge.

Cut textured yarn. Holding 2 strands of eyelash yarn together, knit 6 rows.

Bind off all sts.

Weave in all yarn ends.

HAT
Finished Size: 22" (56 cm) circumference

BODY
Holding 2 strands of eyelash yarn together, cast on 50 sts.

Knit 6 rows.

Cut eyelash yarn. Using one strand of textured yarn, knit each row until Hat measures approximately 7" (18 cm) from cast on edge.

CROWN
Row 1 (Decrease row): (K8, K2 tog) across *(Fig. 4, page 46)*: 45 sts.

Row 2: Knit across.

Row 3 (Decrease row): (K7, K2 tog) across: 40 sts.

Working one less stitch between decreases, continue to decrease 5 sts, every other row, in same manner, 6 times **more**: 10 sts.

Instructions continued on page 16.

Courtney wandered through the store. She'd had no idea there were so many different varieties of yarn. A display scarf knitted in variegated colors was gorgeous, and there was a felted purse, a vest and a sweater.

rainbow poncho

Lydia says this poncho is brilliantly easy. Every row is knit and you change colors when desired. It's a fun project for a beginner and fantastic relaxation for a more advanced knitter.

◼◼◻◻ **EASY**

Lydia's Tip: This Poncho can easily be made smaller or larger by adjusting the number of rows. Adjust yarn required accordingly.

Finished Size: 48" (122 cm) square

MATERIALS

Medium/Worsted Weight Yarn: **MEDIUM 4**
[4 ounces, 110 grams per skein]:
- Light Maroon – 2 skeins
- Dk Purple Heather – 2 skeins
- Special Raspberry – 1 skein
- Salmon – 1 skein
- Orange – 1 skein
- Yellow – 1 skein
- Lt Green Heather – 1 skein
- Periwinkle – 1 skein
- Lt Purple Heather – 1 skein

Two 29" (73.5 cm) or 36" (91.5 cm) Circular knitting needles, size 8 (5 mm) **or** size needed for gauge
1" (2.5 cm) Buttons - 3
Sewing needle and thread

GAUGE: In Garter Stitch, 16 sts = 4" (10 cm)

TRIANGLE (Make 2)

This Poncho is made from two triangles which are knit from the wrist to the shoulder and joined at center back.

Our color sequence is as follows: Light Maroon, Special Raspberry, Salmon, Orange, Yellow, Lt Green Heather, Periwinkle, Lt Purple Heather, and Dk Purple Heather.
Make the stripes as many rows as desired, but not the same each time. Make both Triangles the same.

Cast on 6 sts.

Rows 1 and 2: Knit across.

Row 3: K3, YO *(Fig. 1, page 44)*, knit across.

Repeat Row 3 for pattern until side of Triangle measures approximately 48" (122 cm) **or** desired measurement from forearm to shoulder, changing colors every 1 to 6 rows. As you change colors, knot the ends, leaving a 7" (18 cm) end which will become part of the fringe, ending by working no more than 3 rows of the last color.

Slip sts on first Triangle only onto holding yarn.

Instructions continued on page 16.

FINISHING

Count the number of stitches on the last row of the Triangle and divide that number by two. Subtract 16 stitches for neck. This will be the number of stitches on the back; slip these sts from the holding yarn on the first Triangle onto a second circular needle.

Work 3 needle bind off across back stitches as follows:
Hold pieces with **right** sides together and needles parallel to each other, using the empty end of the circular needle for the left hand needle. Insert the left hand needle as if to **knit** into the first stitch on the front needle **and** into the first stitch on the back needle **(Fig. E)**. Knit these two stitches together and slip them off the needle, ★ Knit the next stitch on each needle together and slip them off the needle. To bind off, insert the left needle into the first stitch on the right needle and lift the first stitch over the second stitch and off the right needle; repeat from ★ across until all of the stitches on the front needle have been bound off.

Fig. E

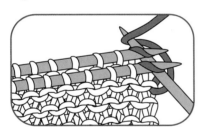

With **right** side facing and beginning at bottom right front edge, bind off remaining sts on right front; pick up 2 sts at joining; slip sts from left front holding yarn onto circular needle and bind off all remaining sts.

Overlap Fronts and sew buttons through both pieces. The buttons may be removed later to turn your Poncho into a Shawl.

Holding three strands together, add Fringe around outer edge matching colors of stripes **(Figs. 13a & b, page 48)**.

Design by Marcia Carpenter for Philosopher Wool.

16

Fur & Bouclé Hat & Scarf continued from page 12.

Cut textured yarn leaving a long end for sewing. Holding 2 strands of eyelash yarn together, knit 2 rows.

Cut yarn leaving a long end for sewing.

FINISHING

Thread yarn needle with end and slip remaining sts onto yarn needle; gather tightly to close Hat and secure.

Weave seam **(Fig. 12, page 47)**.

With Eyelash yarn, make a 2" (5 cm) pom-pom as follows:
Cut a piece of cardboard 3" (7.5 cm) square. Wind the yarn around the cardboard until it is approximately ½" (12 mm) thick in the middle **(Fig. F)**.
Carefully slip the yarn off the cardboard and firmly tie an 18" (45.5 cm) length of yarn around the middle **(Fig. G)**. Leave the ends long enough to attach the pom-pom. Cut the loops on both ends and trim the pom-pom into a smooth ball **(Fig. H)**.
Sew pom-pom to top of Hat.

Fig. F   **Fig. G**   **Fig. H**

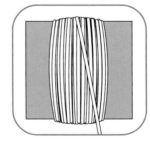  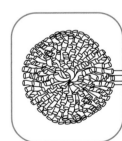

Weave in all yarn ends.

Design by Nancie M. Wiseman.

Courtney's Leg Warmers continued from page 10.

FINISHING
WRAPPED POM-POMS

Make approximately 12 each in 6 different colors.

Thread a tapestry needle with 24" (61 cm) of yarn. Holding one end securely against a small straw or other thin cylindrical object, wrap yarn around straw 18 times, being careful that the loops lie parallel to each other and do not overlap.

Slide the needle under the loops being careful not to split the yarn *(Fig. I)*.

Slide the needle under the loops again *(Fig. J)* and then slide all loops off the straw.

Pull both yarn ends tightly *(Fig. K)*, firming loops into a pom-pom *(Fig. L)*.

Fig. I

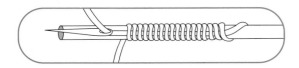

Fig. J

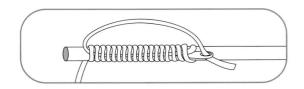

Fig. K   **Fig. L**

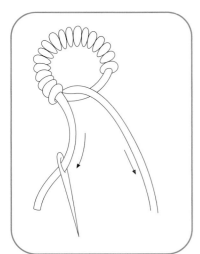

Tie yarn ends into a knot close to pom-pom; do not cut yarn ends.

Arrange 6 pom-poms of each color on each Leg Warmer as desired.

Thread both ends through tapestry needle and pull through to wrong side of Leg Warmer. Bring needle up through center of pom-pom, pull threads over one side of pom-pom and back through to wrong side; repeat pulling threads over opposite side. Tie ends securely in a knot under stitch just made, being careful not to distort shape of pom-pom.

Repeat for each pom-pom.

Weave back seams *(Fig. 12, page 47)*.

17

vera's lacy scarf

Courtney's grandmother likes to share this delicate-looking scarf pattern with her friends. She says that, once you catch the rhythm, your needles almost produce the fabric by themselves.

Lydia's Tip: This scarf can be made to look casual or dressy, depending on the type of yarn used.

Finished Size: 6½" x 71" (16.5 cm x 180.5 cm)

MATERIALS

Medium/Worsted Weight Yarn: **MEDIUM 4**
[2½ ounces, 162 yards, 70 grams, 146 meters per skein]: 3 skeins
Straight knitting needles, size 8 (5 mm)
Yarn needle

GAUGE: In Stockinette Stitch,
18 sts = 4" (10 cm)

SCARF

Cast on 29 sts.

Row 1: Knit across.

Row 2: Purl across.

Row 3: K2, YO *(Fig. 1, page 44)*, K1, [slip 1 as if to **knit**, K2 tog, PSSO *(Fig. 7, page 46)*], K1, YO, ★ K1, P3, K1, YO, K1, slip 1 as if to **knit**, K2 tog, PSSO, K1, YO; repeat from ★ once **more**, K2: 29 sts.

Row 4: P8, K3, P7, K3, P8.

Rows 5-10: Repeat Rows 3 and 4, 3 times.

Row 11: K3, P3, ★ K1, YO, K1, slip 1 as if to **knit**, K2 tog, PSSO, K1, YO, K1, P3; repeat from ★ once **more**, K3: 29 sts.

Row 12: P3, K3, (P7, K3) twice, P3.

Rows 13-18: Repeat Rows 11 and 12, 3 times.

Repeat Rows 3-18 for pattern until Scarf measures approximately 71" (180.5 cm) from cast on edge, ending by working **Row 10 or Row 18**.

Repeat Rows 1 and 2.

Bind off all sts.

Weave in all yarn ends.

My students listened as I showed them a variety of yarns available. I also passed around a gauge to help the class figure out the proper number of stitches to cast on according to the weight of the yarn. The light, fingering style yarn required more stitches, the heavier yarns fewer.

—Lydia

first steps
baby blanket

Every mom knows you can never have too many baby blankets. This refreshing little afghan in springtime colors works up very quickly, and its ever-changing hues are a benefit of using variegated yarn.

■■□□ **EASY**

Lydia's Note: The first stitch on each row is slipped. This gives a nice smooth edge when working the Garter Stitch (knit every row) Border.

Finished Size: 34 1/2" x 45" (87.5 cm x 114.5 cm)

MATERIALS

Medium/Worsted Weight Yarn: **MEDIUM 4**
[2.8 ounces, 130 yards, 80 grams, 119 meters per skein]: 8 skeins
31" (78.5 cm) or 36" (91.5 cm) Circular knitting needle, size 10 (6 mm) **or** size needed for gauge
Yarn needle

GAUGE: In Stockinette Stitch,
14 sts = 4" (10 cm)

BODY

Cast on 121 sts.

When instructed to slip a stitch, always slip as if to **purl** with yarn held to **wrong** side.

Row 1: Knit across.

Rows 2-8: Slip 1, knit across.

Row 9: Slip 1, K5, purl across to last 6 sts, K6.

Row 10: Slip 1, knit across.

Rows 11-13: Slip 1, K5, P1, (K1, P1) across to last 6 sts, K6.

Row 14: Slip 1, knit across.

Row 15: Slip 1, K5, purl across to last 6 sts, K6.

Row 16: Slip 1, K5, K1, (YO, K2 tog) across to last 6 sts (*Fig. 1, page 44 and Fig. 4, page 46)*, K6.

Rows 17-23: Repeat Rows 9-15.

Row 24: Slip 1, K5, (K2 tog, YO) across to last 7 sts, K7.

Repeat Rows 9-24 for pattern until Blanket measures approximately 43 1/2" (110.5 cm) from cast on edge, ending by working **Row 15 or Row 23**.

Last 8 Rows: Slip 1, knit across.

Bind off all sts in knit.

Weave in all yarn ends.

Design by Nona Claus.

I'd given Elise some donated yarn and she was knitting a blanket for the Linus Project at home. Alix had knit a couple of blankets for them, too.
—Lydia

maverick's laprobe

The plaid look on this warm and masculine lap robe is achieved by using two colors to make each strip. Alternating blocks of Stockinette Stitch and Reverse Stockinette Stitch give the design more texture, and a crocheted trim frames each block.

◼◼◻◻ **EASY**

Finished Size: 34 1/2" x 49" (87.5 cm x 125.5 cm)

MATERIALS

Bulky Weight Yarn: **BULKY 5**

[6 ounces, 185 yards, 170 grams, 169 meters per skein]:
Blue – 3 skeins
Variegated – 3 skeins
Tan – 1 skein
Straight knitting needles, size 17 (12.75 mm) **or** size needed for gauge
Crochet hook, size P (10 mm)

Afghan is worked holding two strands of yarn together except for Assembly and Stripes.

GAUGE: In Stockinette Stitch,
7 sts and 10 rows = 4" (10 cm)

PANEL A (Make 3)

With Variegated, cast on 12 sts.

Row 1: Knit across.

Row 2 (Right side): Purl across.

Note: Loop a short piece of yarn around any stitch to mark Row 2 as **right** side and **bottom** edge.

Rows 3-16: Repeat Rows 1 and 2, 7 times (for Reverse Stockinette Stitch).

Row 17: With Blue, purl across.

Row 18: Knit across.

Row 19: Purl across.

Rows 20-32: Repeat Rows 18 and 19, 6 times; then repeat Row 18 once **more** (for Stockinette Stitch).

Lydia's Tip: To omit a different colored ridge on the right side when changing from Stockinette Stitch to Reverse Stockinette Stitch, the first row of the Reverse Stockinette Stitch section is worked by purling across instead of knitting.

Row 33: With Variegated, purl across.

Rows 34-112: Repeat Rows 2-33 twice, then repeat Rows 2-16 once **more**.

Bind off all sts in **knit**.

Instructions continued on page 27.

*E*lise joined her husband in the living room. She sat across from him and unfolded her pattern. She was knitting Maverick a lap robe for times like this. They'd been together a year now, and not once had she regretted remarrying Maverick. Being in love did something for a woman, she decided.

cameron's hooded cardigan

A toddler's world is ever expanding, and he needs a sweater that will give him lots of room to flex and grow. The raglan sleeves on this cardigan allow plenty of ease through the shoulders. The wavy design on the torso is echoed on the sleeves and adds a little color.

■■■□ INTERMEDIATE

Lydia's Tip: The cardigan is worked in one piece from the hood down, which also means there is very little hand sewing to do. The Sleeves are worked on two circular needles using the same method as the socks. You can also use double pointed needles for the Sleeves, if you prefer that method.

Size: 12 months
Finished Chest Measurement: 21" (53.5 cm)

MATERIALS
Medium/Worsted Weight Yarn: **MEDIUM 4**
[3 ounces, 197 yards, 85 grams, 180 meters per skein]: Blue – 2 skeins
[5 ounces, 280 yards, 140 grams, 256 meters per skein]: Variegated – 1 skein
Two 24" (61 cm) or 29" (73.5 cm) Circular knitting needles each, sizes 6 (4 mm) **and** 8 (5 mm) **or** sizes needed for gauge
Markers
18" (45.5 cm) all-purpose zipper
Sewing needle and thread
Yarn needle

GAUGE: With larger size needle,
In Stockinette Stitch,
18 sts and 24 rows = 4" (10 cm)

HOOD
With larger size needle and Blue, cast on 23 sts.

Row 1: K4, purl across.

Row 2 (Right side): Knit across.

Repeat Rows 1 and 2 for pattern until Hood measures approximately 14" (35.5 cm) from cast on edge, ending by working **Row 2**.

NECK RIBBING
To pick up and knit stitches, pick up a stitch *(Figs. 11a & b, page 47)* and place it on the left needle, then knit the stitch.

Joining Row: Turn; add on 4 sts *(Figs. 2a & b, page 44)*, turn, with **right** side of cast on edge facing, pick up and knit 23 sts across: 50 sts.

Change to smaller size needle.

Work in K1, P1 ribbing for 7 rows.

RAGLAN SHAPING
Change to larger size needle.

Lydia's Tip: The knit increase uses one stitch to make two stitches and is formed by working into the front and into the back of the same stitch. You will have two stitches on the right needle for the one stitch worked off the left needle.

Row 1 (Increase row): K8, increase *(Figs. 3a & b, page 45)*, place marker *(see Markers, page 44)*, increase, K5, increase, place marker, increase, K 16, increase, place marker, increase, K5, increase, place marker, increase, K8: 58 sts.

Instructions continued on page 26.

Row 2: Purl across.

Row 3 (Increase row): (Knit across to within one st of marker, increase twice) 4 times, knit across: 66 sts.

Rows 4-26: Repeat Rows 2 and 3, 11 times, then repeat Row 2 once **more**: 154 sts.

BODY

Row 1 (Dividing row): ★ Knit across to marker, turn, add on 4 sts, turn, slip next 33 sts onto holding yarn for Sleeve; repeat from ★ once **more**, knit across: 96 sts.

Row 2: Purl across.

Rows 3-6: With Variegated, work 4 rows in Reverse Stockinette Stitch.

Rows 7-13: With Blue, work 7 rows in Stockinette Stitch.

Rows 14-28: Repeat Rows 3-13 once, then repeat Rows 3-6 once **more**.

With Blue, work in Stockinette Stitch until Body measures approximately 6" (15 cm) from underarm.

BOTTOM RIBBING
Change to smaller size needles.

Work in K1, P1 ribbing for 1" (2.5 cm), ending by working a **wrong** side row.

Bind off all sts in ribbing; do **not** cut yarn.

EDGING
With **right** side facing, pick up and knit 2 sts, bind off one st on the right needle, ★ pick up and knit one st, bind off one st on the right needle; repeat from ★ along entire front opening; finish off.

SLEEVE

With **right** side facing, slip 16 sts from Sleeve holding yarn onto larger size needle, slip remaining 17 sts onto second needle *(see **Knitting in the Round With Two Circular Needles, page 6)**: 33 sts.

When going from one needle to the next, keep the yarn between the first and last stitches snug to prevent a hole.

Rnd 1: Beginning at underarm and using the other end of the first needle, add on 2 sts, knit across first needle, slide sts to the center of the cable; using the other end of the second needle, knit across the second needle, turn; add on 2 sts; turn: 37 sts.

Rnd 2: Knit around.

Rnds 3-6: With Variegated yarn, purl around.

Rnd 7 (Decrease rnd): With Blue, K1, [slip 1 as if to **knit**, K1, PSSO *(Figs. 6a & b, page 46)*], knit around to last 3 sts, K2 tog *(Fig. 4, page 46)*, K1: 35 sts.

Rnds 8-13: Knit around.

Work in same pattern as Body, continuing to decrease every seventh rnd, 3 times **more**: 29 sts.

Work even until Sleeves measures approximately 5¹⁄₂" (14 cm) from underarm.

SLEEVE RIBBING
Change to smaller size needles.

Rnd 1: K2 tog, P1, (K1, P1) across: 28 sts.

Work in ribbing for 1" (2.5 cm).

Bind off all sts in ribbing.

Repeat for second Sleeve.

FINISHING

Sew added on sts at underarm together.

Sew zipper in place, using doubled thread and back stitching.

Weave in all yarn ends.

Design by Laura Early.

Maverick's Laprobe continued from page 22.

PANEL B (Make 2)

With Tan, cast on 12 sts.

Row 1 (Right side)**:** Knit across.

Note: Mark Row 1 as **right** side and **bottom** edge.

Row 2: Purl across.

Rows 3-16: Repeat Rows 1 and 2, 7 times (for Stockinette Stitch).

Row 17: With Variegated, knit across.

Row 18: Knit across.

Row 19: Purl across.

Rows 20-32: Repeat Rows 18 and 19, 6 times; then repeat Row 18 once **more** (for Reverse Stockinette Stitch).

Row 33: With Tan, knit across.

Rows 34-112: Repeat Rows 2-33 twice, then repeat Rows 2-16 once **more**.

Bind off all sts in **purl**.

ASSEMBLY

Join Panels in following sequence:
Panel A, (Panel B, Panel A) twice.
With **right** sides together and marker at same end, using crochet hook and working in end of rows through **both** thicknesses, join one strand of Variegated with slip st in Row 1 *(see Crochet Stitches, page 48)*; slip st in next row and in each row across; finish off.
Join remaining Panels in same manner.

TRIM

With **right** side of one long edge facing, using crochet hook and working in end of rows, join two strands of Blue with sc in end of first row; ch 1, (skip next row, sc in next row, ch 1) across to last 3 rows, skip next row, sc in last 2 rows; finish off.

Repeat across opposite long edge.

HORIZONTAL STRIPES

Work Horizontal Stripe, along first color change row across all Panels, as follows:

With **right** side facing and Blue, make a slip knot on hook; keeping working yarn to **wrong** side, slip st around first st on first Panel and around each st across to last st on last Panel; finish off.

Repeat across each remaining color change rows.

VERTICAL STRIPES

Work Vertical Stripe, along joining between Panels, as follows:

With **right** side facing and Blue; make a slip knot on hook; keeping working yarn to **wrong** side, slip st in Row 1 and in each row across; finish off.

Repeat along each remaining joining.

Holding six 18" (45.5 cm) strands of Blue together and using photo as a guide for placement, add Fringe to both short ends *(Figs. 13a & b, page 48)*.
It may be helpful to knot the ends to prevent fraying.

fair isle hat & scarf

Fair Isle is a classic style of knitting that every creative person should try at least once. This hat and scarf are a great place to begin. It's also best to start with a practice swatch. Lydia predicts that you will be surprised at how much you like knitting this pretty set.

◼◼◼◻ **INTERMEDIATE**

MATERIALS

Fine/Sport Weight Yarn: 🅵🅸🅽🅴 **2**

[5 ounces, 455 yards, 140 grams, 416 meters per skein]:

- Pink – 1 skein
- Variegated – 1 skein
- White – 1 skein
- Dk Pink – 10 yards

Straight knitting needles, sizes 3 (3.25 mm) **and** 5 (3.75 mm) **or** sizes needed for gauge

Crochet hook (for fringe)

Tapestry needle

GAUGE: With larger size needles, in Stockinette Stitch, 24 sts and 32 rows = 4" (10 cm)

HAT

Size	Finished Measurement
Small	16$\frac{1}{2}$" (42 cm)
Medium	18$\frac{1}{2}$" (47 cm)
Large	20" (51 cm)

Size Note: Instructions are written for size Small with sizes Medium and Large in braces { }. Instructions will be easier to read if you circle all the numbers pertaining to your size. If only one number is given, it applies to all sizes.

RIBBING

With Pink and smaller size needles, cast on 102{112-122} sts.

Work in K1, P1 ribbing for 1$\frac{1}{4}$" (3 cm).

BODY

Change to larger size needles.

Working in Stockinette Stitch (knit one row, purl one row) and beginning with a knit row, work 2 rows with Variegated then 2 rows with Pink.

Instructions continued on page 30.

She had that look in her eye, a look I recognized. Those of us who are addicted to yarn seem to share it. Jacqueline was among my best customers; she could afford to buy as much yarn as she wanted, and she did, without restraint.
—Lydia

Follow Chart, page 31.

Beginning with Pink, work even alternating 2 rows of Pink with 2 rows of Variegated until Hat measures approximately 6{6½-7}"/ 15{16.5-18} cm from cast on edge, ending by working a **purl** row.

CROWN
Maintain established color sequence.

Row 1: K2, ★ K2 tog (*Fig. 4, page 46*), K8{9-10}; repeat from ★ across: 92{102-112} sts.

Row 2: P2, ★ P2 tog (*Fig. 8, page 46*), P7{8-9}; repeat from ★ across: 82{92-102} sts.

Row 3: K2, ★ K2 tog, K6{7-8}; repeat from ★ across: 72{82-92} sts.

Continue to decrease 10 sts each row, working one less st between decreases until 20 sts remain; at end of last row, cut yarn leaving a long end for sewing.

FINISHING
Thread yarn needle with end pulling it even to make a double strand; slip remaining sts onto yarn needle; gather tightly to close Hat and secure.

Add Duplicate Stitch as indicated on Chart (*Figs. 10a & b, page 47*).

Weave seam (*Fig. 12, page 47*).

Weave in all yarn ends.

SCARF
Size	Finished Measurements
Small	4¼" x 40" (11 cm x 101.5 cm)
Large	5" x 50" (12.5 cm x 127 cm)

Size Note: Instructions are written for size Small with size Large in braces { }. Instructions will be easier to read if you circle all the numbers pertaining to your size. If only one number is given, it applies to all sizes.

BODY
With Pink and larger size needles, cast on 52{62} sts.

Beginning with a knit row, work 14 rows in Stockinette Stitch (knit one row, purl one row), alternating 2 rows of Pink with 2 rows of Variegated.

Follow Chart, page 31.

Beginning with Pink, work even alternating 2 rows of Pink with 2 rows of Variegated until Scarf measures approximately 36{46}"/91.5{117} cm from cast on edge, ending by working a **knit** row with Pink.

Follow Chart.

Beginning with Pink, work even for 14 rows, alternating 2 rows of Pink with 2 rows of Variegated.

Bind off all sts.

FINISHING
Add Duplicate Stitch as indicated on Chart (*Figs. 10a & b, page 47*).

With **right** sides together, fold Body in half lengthwise and weave side seam (*Fig. 12, page 47*); turn right side out.

Weave in all yarn ends.

Holding six 12" (30.5 cm) strands of Pink together and working through both layers, add Fringe to both ends (*Figs. 13a & b, page 48*).

CHART

On Row 9, you can knit with both Pink and Dk Pink, or add Dk Pink Duplicate Stitch later.

On **right** side rows, follow Chart from **right** to **left**;
on **wrong** side rows, follow Chart from **left** to **right**.

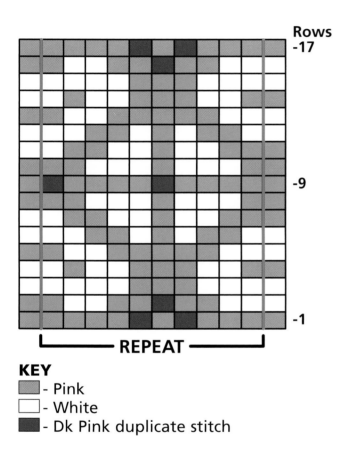

Rows
-17

-9

-1

REPEAT

KEY
- Pink
- White
- Dk Pink duplicate stitch

Design by Zara Zsido.

FAIR ISLE KNITTING

Fair Isle knitting is a Stockinette Stitch technique that uses two colors across a row. The English method of knitting (holding the yarn with the right hand) and the Continental method (holding the yarn with the left hand) can be combined for ease in changing colors. Stranding is also used, which is a method in which the color not in use is carried across the wrong side of the fabric.

To avoid carrying the yarn across 5 stitches, twist the carried color at its midpoint with the yarn in use. Make sure the carried yarn doesn't show on the right side or tighten the tension. Drop the color you are using, lay the other color to your left on top of it, pick up the color you were using and continue working. The unused color is attached to the fabric. Spread your stitches on the right hand needle as you knit so that you will have the correct tension on the yarn that is being carried. The stitches should be spread as much as the approximate gauge, so that the yarn carried will lie flat against the fabric. Carrying the strand slightly too loose is better than too tight, but be careful not to provide too much yarn as the stitches at end of the color section will enlarge. It's important to maintain the elasticity of the fabric.

The fabric should look smooth and even on the right side without a puckered uneven appearance. The strands on the wrong side should lie flat without pulling the fabric or distorting the shape of the stitches. If the strands are pulled too tight, the gauge will also be too tight.

FOLLOWING A CHART

The chart shows each stitch as a square indicating what color each stitch should be. Only one pattern repeat is given on the chart, and it is indicated by a heavy vertical line and a bracketed indication. This section is to be repeated across the row. There is an extra stitch on each side of the repeat, indicating the first and last stitch of the row. These are edge stitches that will be woven into the seam, allowing the pattern to be continuous.

annie's pullover

So soft and feminine, Annie's Pullover is a split turtleneck design that Bethanne first made with cashmere yarn, but of course you can use whatever yarn you please. The ribbing is knit-two, purl-two — a classic pattern.

■■■□ INTERMEDIATE

Size	Finished Bust Measurement
X-Small	32¹/₂" (82.5 cm)
Small	36" (91.5 cm)
Medium	39¹/₂" (100.5 cm)
Large	43" (109 cm)

Size Note: Instructions are written for size X-Small with sizes Small, Medium and Large in braces { }. Instructions will be easier to read if you circle all the numbers pertaining to your size. If only one number is given, it applies to all sizes.

MATERIALS
Medium/Worsted Weight Yarn: **MEDIUM 4**
[1³/₄ ounces, 136.5 yards, 50 grams,
    125 meters per skein]: 11{12-13-14} skeins
Straight knitting needles, sizes 3 (3.25 mm)
    and 5 (3.75 cm) **or** sizes needed
    for gauge
Stitch holders – 2
Yarn needle

GAUGE: With larger size needles,
    in Body pattern,
    20 sts and 28 rows = 4" (10 cm)

Gauge Swatch: 4" (10 cm) square
With larger size needles, cast on 20 sts.
Work same as Body for 28 rows.
Bind off all sts in pattern.

BACK
RIBBING
With smaller size needles, cast on
82{90-98-110} sts.

Row 1: P2, (K2, P2) across.

Row 2: K2, (P2, K2) across.

Repeat Rows 1 and 2 until ribbing measures approximately 3" (7.5 cm) from cast on edge, ending by working **Row 1**.

Last Row: Work across in established ribbing, increasing 1{2-3-0} sts *(see Zeros, page 45)* evenly spaced across *(see Increases and Increasing Evenly, page 45)*: 83{92-101-110} sts.

Instructions continued on page 38.

"That pink cashmere sweater is for me?" Annie cried, absolutely delighted. "Mom, I'm so excited you're knitting it for me."

Bethanne liked the fact that she could produce something both useful and beautiful. It seemed like a hundred years ago that her teenage daughter had taken the initiative and signed Bethanne up for the knitting class.

cody's dinosaur sweater

What future archeologist wouldn't adore this dinosaur sweater? The design trails around the torso, with the tail of the dinosaur ending on the back of the pullover. If you like, add a bead to the front for the dinosaur's eye.

■■■□ INTERMEDIATE

Size	Chest Measurement	Finished Chest Measurement
4	24" (61 cm)	27" (68.5 cm)
6	25½" (65 cm)	29½" (75 cm)
8	27" (68.5 cm)	31" (78.5 cm)

Size Note: Instructions are written for size 4, with sizes 6 and 8 in braces { }. Instructions will be easier to read if you circle all the numbers pertaining to your size. If only one number is given, it applies to all sizes.

MATERIALS

Medium/Worsted Weight Yarn: **MEDIUM 4**
[3½ ounces, 174 yards, 100 grams,
   159 meters per skein]:
   Main Color (Blue) – 4{4-5} skeins
   Brown – 1 skein
Straight knitting needles, sizes 4 (3.5 mm)
   and 6 (4 mm) or sizes needed for gauge
16" (40.5 cm) Circular needle, size 4 (3.5 mm)
Bobbins
Stitch holders – 2
Marker
Black bead for eye
Yarn needle

GAUGE: With larger size needles,
   in Stockinette Stitch,
   20 sts and 26 rows = 4" (10 cm)

Lydia's Tip: The larger size needles are used for the Front and Back ribbing. The ribbing is intended to only pull in slightly, helping the dinosaur to be visible and not distorted.

SLEEVE (Make 2)
RIBBING

With Main Color and smaller size needles, cast on 30{32-32} sts.

Work in K1, P1 ribbing for 2{2-2½}"/5{5-6.5} cm increasing 4 sts evenly spaced across last row *(see Increases and Increasing Evenly, page 45)*: 34{36-36} sts.

BODY

Change to larger size needles.

Row 1 (Right side)**:** Knit across.

Row 2: Purl across.

Rows 3 and 4: Repeat Rows 1 and 2.

Row 5 (Increase row)**:** K1, increase, knit across to last 2 sts, increase, K1: 36{38-38} sts.

Working in Stockinette Stitch, continue to increase one stitch at **each** edge in same manner, every fourth row, 3{0-5} times **more** *(see Zeros, page 45)*; then increase every sixth row, 5{8-5} times: 52{54-58} sts.

Instructions continued on page 36.

This was an attractive shop, well-designed and not overcrowded with yarn. Elise liked that she could see over the top of each display case. There were projects displayed on top of the cases, cleverly arranged on wire frames. Her eye was drawn to a sweater with a dinosaur knit into the front. Perhaps one day she'd make it for her grandsons.

35

Work even until Sleeve measures approximately 10½{11¾-12}"/26.5{30-30.5} cm from cast on edge **or desired length to underarm**, ending by working a **purl** row.

SLEEVE CAP
Rows 1 and 2: Bind off 2{4-4} sts, work across: 48{46-50} sts.

Row 3 (Decrease row)**:** K1, [slip 1 as if to **knit**, K1, PSSO *(Figs. 6a & b, page 46)*], knit across to last 3 sts, K2 tog *(Fig. 4, page 46)*, K1: 46{44-48} sts.

Row 4: Purl across.

Repeat Rows 3 and 4, 7{9-10} times: 32{26-28} sts.

Bind off 4{3-3} sts at the beginning of the next 4 rows, work across: 16{14-16} sts.

Bind off 4{3-4} sts at the beginning of the next 2 rows, work across: 8 sts.

Bind off remaining sts.

FRONT
RIBBING
With Main Color and larger size needles, cast on 70{76-80} sts.

Work in K1, P1 ribbing for 1½{1½-2}"/4{4-5} cm.

BODY
Beginning with a **knit** row, work 4 rows in Stockinette Stitch.

Lydia's Tip: When changing colors, always pick up the new color yarn from beneath the dropped yarn and keep the color which has just been worked to the left. This will prevent holes in the finished piece. Take extra care to keep your tension even. Use bobbins to hold the small amount of yarn needed to work each color change and also to keep the different color yarns from tangling. You'll need to wind a bobbin for each color change, using as many bobbins as necessary to avoid carrying the yarn across the back.

FRONT CHART

KEY
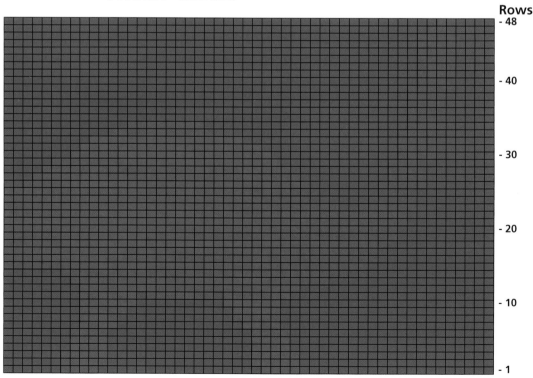

- Main Color (Blue)
- Brown

On **right** side rows, follow Chart from **right** to **left**; on **wrong** side rows, follow Chart from **left** to **right**.

Next Row: Knit across 19{25-29} sts, place marker to mark edge of Chart **(see Markers, page 44)**, knit across following Front Chart.

Continue to follow Chart.

Work even until Front measures approximately 10¼{11¼-12¼}"/26{28.5-31} cm from cast on edge, ending by working a **purl** row.

ARMHOLE SHAPING

Rows 1 and 2: Bind off 2{4-4} sts, work across: 66{68-72} sts.

Row 3 (Decrease row): K1, slip 1 as if to **knit**, K1, PSSO, knit across to last 3 sts, K2 tog, K1: 64{66-70} sts.

Row 4: Purl across.

Repeat Rows 3 and 4, 6{5-6} times: 52{56-58} sts.

Work even until Armholes measure approximately 3¼{3½-4}"/8.5{9-10} cm, ending by working a **knit** row.

NECK SHAPING

Both sides of Neck are worked at the same time, using separate yarn for **each** side.

Row 1: Purl 19{21-21} sts, slip next 14{14-16} sts onto st holder; with second yarn, purl across: 19{21-21} sts **each** side.

Row 2 (Decrease row): Knit across to within 2 sts of neck edge, K2 tog; with second yarn, slip 1 as if to **knit**, K1, PSSO, knit across: 18{20-20} sts **each** side.

Row 3 (Decrease row): Purl across to within 2 sts of neck edge, P2 tog **(Fig. 8, page 46)**; with second yarn, SSP **(Fig. 9, page 47)**, purl across: 17{19-19} sts **each** side.

Row 4 (Decrease row): Knit across to within 2 sts of neck edge, K2 tog; with second yarn, slip 1 as if to **knit**, K1, PSSO, knit across: 16{18-18} sts **each** side.

Row 5: Purl across; with second yarn, purl across.

Rows 6-9: Repeat Rows 4 and 5 twice: 14{16-16} sts **each** side.

Work even until Armholes measure approximately 5¼{5¾-6¼}"/13.5{14.5-16} cm, ending by working a **knit** row.

SHOULDER SHAPING

Rows 1 and 2: Bind off 4{5-5} sts, work across; with second yarn, work across: 10{11-11} sts **each** side.

Rows 3 and 4: Bind off 5 sts, work across; with second yarn, work across: 5{6-6} sts **each** side.

Row 5: Bind off remaining sts on first side; with second yarn, work across.

Bind off remaining sts.

BACK
RIBBING

With Main Color and larger size needles, cast on 70{76-80} sts.

Work in K1, P1 ribbing for 1½{1½-2}"/4{4-5} cm.

BODY

Beginning with a **knit** row, work 15 rows in Stockinette Stitch.

Next Row: Purl across 39{45-49} sts, place marker to mark edge of Chart, purl across following Back Chart.

Continue to follow Chart.

BACK CHART

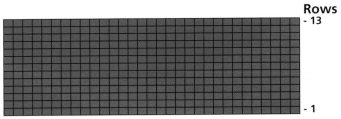

Rows - 13

- 1

Instructions continued on page 38.

37

Work even until Back measures same as Front to Armholes, ending by working a **purl** row.

ARMHOLE SHAPING
Work Shaping same as Front, then work even until Armholes measure same as Front to Shoulder Shaping, ending by working a **knit** row: 52{56-58} sts.

SHOULDER SHAPING
Rows 1 and 2: Bind off 4{5-5} sts, work across: 44{46-48} sts.

Rows 3 and 4: Bind off 5 sts, work across: 34{36-38} sts.

Rows 5 and 6: Bind off 5{6-6} sts, work across: 24{24-26} sts.

Slip remaining sts onto st holder.

FINISHING
Sew bead to dinosaur for eye.

Sew shoulder seams.

NECK RIBBING
With **right** side facing, Main Color, and using circular needle, knit 24{24-26} sts from Back st holder, pick up 17{19-19} sts evenly spaced along Left Neck edge (*Figs. 11a & b, page 47*), knit 14{14-16} sts from Front st holder, pick up 17{19-19} sts evenly spaced along Right Neck edge, place marker to mark beginning of round: 72{76-80} sts.

Work in K1, P1 ribbing around for 1" (2.5 cm).

Bind off all sts **loosely** in ribbing.

Sew Sleeves to sweater, placing center of Sleeve Cap at shoulder seam and matching bound off stitches.

Weave underarm and side in one continuous seam (*Fig. 12, page 47*).

Weave in all yarn ends.

38

Annie's Pullover continued from page 32.

BODY
Change to larger size needles.

Row 1: K3, P1 tbl (*Fig. M*), P3, P1 tbl, (K4, P1 tbl, P3, P1 tbl) across to last 3 sts, K3.

Fig. M

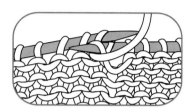

Row 2 (Right side)**:** P3, K1 tbl, K3, K1 tbl, (P4, K1 tbl, K3, K1 tbl) across to last 3 sts, P3.

Repeat Rows 1 and 2 for pattern until Back measures approximately 25" (63.5 cm) from cast on edge, ending by working **Row 1**.

SHOULDER SHAPING
Rows 1-4: Bind off 11{13-15-17} sts, work across in pattern: 39{40-41-42} sts.

Slip remaining sts onto st holder.

FRONT
Work same as Back until Front measures approximately 22$\frac{1}{2}$" (57 cm) from cast on edge, ending by working a **wrong** side row.

NECK SHAPING
Both sides of Neck are worked at the same time, using separate yarn for **each** side. Maintain established pattern throughout.

Row 1: Work across 35{39-43-47} sts, slip next 13{14-15-16} sts onto st holder; with second yarn, work across: 35{39-43-47} sts **each** side.

Rows 2 and 3: Work across; with second yarn, bind of 4 sts, work across: 31{35-39-43} sts **each** side.

Rows 4 and 5: Work across; with second yarn, bind of 3 sts, work across: 28{32-36-40} sts **each** side.

Rows 6 and 7: Work across; with second yarn, bind of 2 sts, work across: 26{30-34-38} sts **each** side.

Row 8 (Decrease row): Work across to within 2 sts of neck edge, decrease *(see Decreases, pages 46 and 47)*; with second yarn, decrease, work across: 25{29-33-37} sts **each** side.

Row 9: Work across; with second yarn, work across.

Rows 10-15: Repeat Rows 8 and 9, 3 times: 22{26-30-34} sts **each** side.

Work even until Front measures same as Back to Shoulder Shaping, ending by working a **wrong** side row.

SHOULDER SHAPING
Rows 1 and 2: Bind off 11{13-15-17} sts, work across; with second yarn, work across: 11{13-15-17} sts **each** side.

Row 3: Bind off remaining sts on first side; with second yarn, work across.

Bind off remaining sts.

SLEEVE (Make 2)
RIBBING
With smaller size needles, cast on 42{42-52-52} sts.

Work same as Back, increasing 5{5-4-4} sts on last row: 47{47-56-56} sts.

BODY
Change to larger size needles.

Work in pattern same as Back, increasing one stitch at **each** edge, every fourth row, 6{17-12-22} times; then increase every sixth row, 13{5-7-0} times **more**: 85{91-94-100} sts.

Work even until Sleeve measures approximately 19½{19-18-17½}"/49.5{48.5-45.5-44.5} cm from cast on edge.

Bind off remaining sts in pattern.

FINISHING
Sew right shoulder seam.

COLLAR
With **right** side facing and using smaller size needles, pick up 23{24-25-26} sts evenly spaced along left Front Neck edge *(Figs. 11a & b, page 47)*, slip 13{14-15-16} sts from Front st holder onto empty point and knit across, pick up 23{24-25-26} sts evenly spaced along right Front Neck edge, slip 39{40-41-42} sts from Back st holder onto empty point and knit across: 98{102-106-110} sts.

Work in K2, P2 ribbing same as Back for 4" (10 cm).

Change to larger size needles.

Work in established ribbing until Collar measures approximately 8" (20.5 cm).

Bind off all sts **loosely** in ribbing.

Sew left shoulder seam.

Sew Sleeves to sweater, placing center of Sleeve at shoulder seam and beginning 8½{9-9½-10}"/ 21.5{23-24-25.5} cm down from seam.

Weave underarm and side in one continuous seam *(Fig. 12, page 47)*.

close-fitting vest

Youthful designs like this vest tend to be worn close to the body, so you'll want to be sure of the size needed before you begin knitting. It's a perfect gift for a fashion-conscious teen — don't be surprised if she asks for one in each of her favorite colors!

◖◖◖◻ **INTERMEDIATE**

Size	Finished Bust Measurement
32	32½" (82.5 cm)
34	35" (89 cm)
36	37" (94 cm)
38	39½" (100.5 cm)
40	42" (106.5 cm)
42	43" (109 cm)

Size Note: Instructions are written with sizes 32, 34, and 36 in the first set of braces { }, and sizes 38, 40, and 42 in the second set of braces. Instructions will be easier to read if you circle all the numbers pertaining to your size. If only one number is given, it applies to all sizes.

MATERIALS
Medium/Worsted Weight Yarn: (4) **MEDIUM**
[6 ounces, 350 yards, 170 grams, 320 meters per skein]: 2 skeins
Straight knitting needles, sizes 6 (4 mm) **and** 8 (5 cm) **or** sizes needed for gauge
16" (40.5 cm) Circular needle, size 6 (4 mm)
Stitch holders – 2
Marker
Yarn needle

GAUGE: With larger size needles, in Stockinette Stitch, 18 sts and 24 rows = 4" (10 cm)

BACK
RIBBING
With smaller size needles, cast on {66-72-76}{82-88-90} sts.

Work in K1, P1 ribbing for 5" (12.5 cm), increasing 9 sts evenly spaced across last row *(see Increases and Increasing Evenly, page 45)*: {75-81-85}{91-97-99} sts.

BODY
Change to larger size needles.

Row 1 (Right side)**:** K{4-4-3}{3-3-4} sts, P1, (K5, P1) across to last {4-4-3}{3-3-4} sts, knit across.

Row 2: Purl across.

Repeat Rows 1 and 2 for pattern until Back measures approximately 10" (25.5 cm) from cast on edge, ending by working a **purl** row.

ARMHOLE SHAPING
Maintain established pattern throughout.

Rows 1 and 2: Bind off {9-9-10}{10-11-11} sts, work across: {57-63-65}{71-75-77} sts.

Instructions continued on page 42.

Row 3 (Decrease row)**:** Decrease *(see Decreases, pages 46 and 47)*, work across to last 2 sts, decrease: {55-61-63}{69-73-75} sts.

Row 4: Purl across.

Rows 5-14: Repeat Rows 3 and 4, 5 times: [45-51-53]{59-63-65} sts.

Work even until Armholes measure approximately {7$\frac{1}{2}$-8-8$\frac{1}{2}$}{9-9$\frac{1}{2}$-10}" /{19-20.5-21.5}{23-24-25.5} cm, ending by working a **purl** row.

SHOULDER SHAPING
Rows 1 and 2: Bind off {6-7-7}{8-9-9} sts, work across: {33-37-39}{43-45-47} sts.

Slip remaining sts onto st holder.

FRONT
Work same as Back through Row 14 of Armhole Shaping: {45-51-53}{59-63-65} sts.

NECK SHAPING
Both sides of Neck are worked at the same time, using separate yarn for **each** side. Maintain established pattern throughout.

Row 1: Work across {12-13-14}{15-17-16} sts, slip next {21-25-25}{29-29-33} sts onto st holder; with second yarn, work across: {12-13-14}{15-17-16} sts **each** side.

Row 2: Work across; with second yarn, work across.

Row 3 (Decrease row)**:** Work across to within 2 sts of Neck edge, derease; with second yarn, decrease, work across: {11-12-13}{14-16-15} sts **each** side.

Repeat Rows 2 and 3, {5-5-6}{6-7-6} times: {6-7-7}{8-9-9} sts **each** side.

Work even until Front measures same as Back to Neck, ending by working a **wrong** side row.

Bind off all sts.

FINISHING
Sew shoulder seams.

ARMHOLE RIBBING
With **right** side facing and using smaller size needles, pick up {78-82-88}{92-98-102} sts evenly spaced across *(Figs. 11a & b, page 47)*.

Work in K1, P1 ribbing for 3 rows.

Bind off all sts in ribbing.

Repeat for second Armhole.

NECK RIBBING
With **right** side facing, slip {33-37-39}{43-45-47} sts from Back st holder onto circular needle and knit across, pick up {30-34-38}{40-44-46} sts evenly spaced along Left Neck edge, slip {21-25-25}{29-29-33} sts from Front st holder onto empty point and knit across, pick up {30-34-38}{40-44-46} sts evenly spaced along Right Neck edge, place marker to mark beginning of round: {114-130-140}{152-162-172} sts.

Work in K1, P1 ribbing for 3 rnds.

Bind off all sts **loosely** in ribbing.

Weave side seams *(Fig. 12, page 47)*.

Weave in all yarn ends.

thank you for helping
warm up
america!

Warm Up America! was started in 1991 by a Wisconsin yarn retailer named Evie Rosen. Evie decided to help the homeless by asking her customers, friends, and community to knit or crochet 7" x 9" blocks that would be joined into afghans. The efforts of those original contributors spread across the nation. To date, more than 80,000 afghans have been donated to battered women's shelters, victims of natural disaster, the homeless, and many others who are in need.

With your purchase of this *Knit Along with Debbie Macomber* pattern book, you have already helped the Warm Up America! Foundation. Debbie is generously donating all her profits from the sale of this pattern book to Warm Up America! And Leisure Arts, Inc. is also donating a portion of its proceeds.

But there is still so much more **you** can do to help, and with so little effort. Debbie urges everyone who uses the patterns in this book to take a few minutes to knit a 7" x 9" block for this worthy cause. Please take time to create a block for Warm Up America!, and ask your friends to get involved, as well.

If you are able to provide a completed afghan, Warm Up America! requests that you donate it directly to your local chapter of the American Red Cross or to any charity or social services agency in your community. If you require assistance in assembling the blocks into an afghan, please include your name and address inside the packaging and ship your 7" x 9" blocks to:

Warm Up America! Foundation
2500 Lowell Road
Ranlo, NC 28054

Remember, just a little bit of yarn can make a big difference to someone in need!

Basic patchwork afghans are made of forty-nine 7" x 9" (18 cm x 23 cm) rectangular blocks that are sewn together. Any pattern stitch can be used for the rectangle. Use acrylic medium/worsted weight yarn and size 8 (5 mm) straight knitting needles or size needed to obtain the gauge of 9 stitches to 2" (5 cm).

ABBREVIATIONS

ch(s)	chain(s)
cm	centimeters
K	knit
mm	millimeters
P	purl
PSSO	pass slipped stitch(es) over
Rnd(s)	round(s)
sc	single crochet(s)
SSK	slip, slip, knit
st(s)	stitch(es)
tbl	through back loop
tog	together
YO	yarn over

★ — work instructions following ★ as many **more** times as indicated in addition to the first time.

( ) or [ ] — work enclosed instructions **as many** times as specified by the number immediately following **or** work all enclosed instructions in the stitch or space indicated **or** contains explanatory remarks.

GAUGE

Exact gauge is **essential** for proper size. Before beginning your project, make a sample swatch in the yarn and needle specified in the individual instructions. After completing the swatch, measure it, counting your stitches and rows carefully. If your swatch is larger or smaller than specified, **make another, changing needle size to get the correct gauge**. Keep trying until you find the size needles that will give you the specified gauge. Once proper gauge is obtained, measure width of project approximately every 3" (7.5 cm) to be sure gauge remains consistent.

MARKERS

As a convenience to you, we have used markers to help distinguish the beginning of a pattern. Place markers as instructed. You may use purchased markers or tie a length of contrasting color yarn around the needle. When you reach a marker on each row, slip it from the left needle to the right needle; remove it when no longer needed.

YARN OVER

Bring the yarn forward **between** the needles, then back **over** the top of the right hand needle, so that it is now in position to knit the next stitch (*Fig. 1*).

Fig. 1

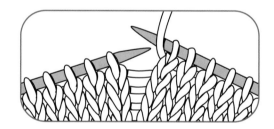

ADDING NEW STITCHES

Insert the right needle into the stitch as if to **knit**, yarn over and pull loop through (*Fig. 2a*), insert left needle into loop just worked from front to back and slip it onto the left needle (*Fig. 2b*). Repeat for required number of stitches.

Fig. 2a

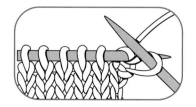

Fig. 2b

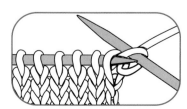

KNIT & CROCHET TERMINOLOGY	
UNITED STATES	**INTERNATIONAL**
gauge =	tension
bind off =	cast off
yarn over (YO) =	yarn forward (yfwd) **or**
	yarn around needle (yrn)
slip stitch (slip st) =	single crochet (sc)
single crochet (sc) =	double crochet (dc)

YARN WEIGHTS						
Yarn Weight Symbol & Names	SUPER FINE **1**	FINE **2**	LIGHT **3**	MEDIUM **4**	BULKY **5**	SUPER BULKY **6**
Type of Yarns in Category	Sock, Fingering Baby	Sport, Baby	DK, Light Worsted	Worsted, Afghan, Aran	Chunky, Craft, Rug	Bulky, Roving

SKILL LEVELS		
●□□□ BEGINNER		Projects for first-time knitters using basic knit and purl stitches. Minimal shaping.
●■□□ EASY		Projects using basic stitches, repetitive stitch patterns, simple color changes, and simple shaping and finishing.
●■■□ INTERMEDIATE		Projects with a variety of stitches, such as basic cables and lace, simple intarsia, double-pointed needles and knitting in the round needle techniques, mid-level shaping and finishing.
●■■■ EXPERIENCED		Projects using advanced techniques and stitches, such as short rows, fair isle, more intricate intarsia, cables, lace patterns, and numerous color changes.

KNITTING NEEDLES															
U.S.	0	1	2	3	4	5	6	7	8	9	10	10½	11	13	15	17
U.K.	13	12	11	10	9	8	7	6	5	4	3	2	1	00	000	---
Metric - mm	2	2.25	2.75	3.25	3.5	3.75	4	4.5	5	5.5	6	6.5	8	9	10	12.75

ALUMINUM CROCHET HOOKS													
U.S.	B-1	C-2	D-3	E-4	F-5	G-6	H-8	I-9	J-10	K-10½	N	P	Q
Metric - mm	2.25	2.75	3.25	3.5	3.75	4	5	5.5	6	6.5	9	10	15

KNIT INCREASE

Knit the next stitch but do **not** slip the old stitch off the left needle (*Fig. 3a*). Insert the right needle into the **back** loop of the **same** stitch and knit it (*Fig. 3b*), then slip the old stitch off the left needle.

Fig. 3a

Fig. 3b

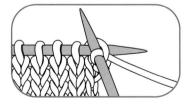
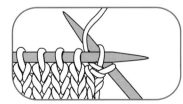

INCREASING EVENLY

Add one to the number of increases required and divide that number into the number of stitches on the needle. Subtract one from the result and the new number is the approximate number of stitches to be worked between each increase. Adjust the number as needed.

ZEROS

To consolidate the length of an involved pattern, Zeros are sometimes used so that all sizes can be combined. For example, increase every fourth row 3{0-5} time(s) means the first size would increase 3 times, the second size would do nothing, and the largest size would increase 5 times.

DECREASES
KNIT 2 TOGETHER
(abbreviated K2 tog)

Insert the right needle into the **front** of the first two stitches on the left needle as if to **knit** *(Fig. 4)*, then **knit** them together as if they were one stitch.

Fig. 4

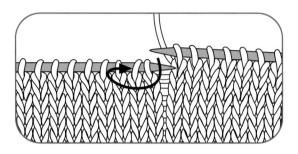

SLIP, SLIP, KNIT
(abbreviated SSK)

With yarn in back of work, separately slip two stitches as if to **knit** *(Fig. 5a)*. Insert the **left** needle into the **front** of both slipped stitches *(Fig. 5b)* and knit them together as if they were one stitch *(Fig. 5c)*.

Fig. 5a   **Fig. 5b**

Fig. 5c

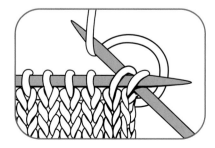

SLIP 1, KNIT 1, PASS SLIPPED STITCH OVER
(abbreviated slip 1, K1, PSSO)

Slip one stitch as if to **knit** *(Fig. 6a)*. Knit the next stitch. With the left needle, bring the slipped stitch over the knit stitch *(Fig. 6b)* and off the needle.

Fig. 6a   **Fig. 6b**

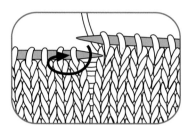 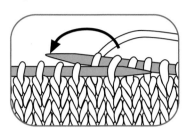

SLIP 1, KNIT 2 TOGETHER, PASS SLIPPED STITCH OVER
(abbreviated slip 1, K2 tog, PSSO)

Slip one stitch as if to **knit** *(Fig. 6a)*, then knit the next two stitches together *(Fig. 4)*. With the left needle, bring the slipped stitch over the stitch just made *(Fig. 7)* and off the needle.

Fig. 7

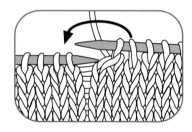

PURL 2 TOGETHER
(abbreviated P2 tog)

Insert the right needle into the **front** of the first two stitches on the left needle as if to **purl** *(Fig. 8)*, then **purl** them together as if they were one stitch.

Fig. 8

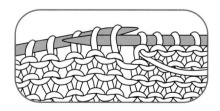

SLIP, SLIP, PURL
(abbreviated SSP)

Separately slip two stitches as if to **knit** (*Fig. 5a, page 46*). Place these two stitches back onto the left needle. Insert the **right** needle into the **back** of both slipped stitches from **back** to **front** (*Fig. 9*) and purl them together as if they were one stitch.

Fig. 9

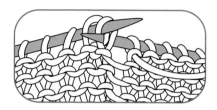

DUPLICATE STITCH

Thread a tapestry needle with an 18" (45.5 cm) length of yarn. Each square on the chart represents one knit stitch. Each knit stitch forms a V. With **right** side facing, bring the needle up from the wrong side at the base of the V, leaving an end to be woven in later. The needle should always go **between** the strands of yarn. Follow the right side of the V up and insert the needle from right to left under the legs of the V immediately above it, keeping the yarn on top of the stitch (*Fig. 10a*), and draw through. Follow the left side of the V back down to the base and insert the needle back through the bottom of the same stitch where the first stitch began (*Fig. 10b, Duplicate Stitch completed*).

Continuing to follow the chart, repeat for each stitch, keeping tension even with tension of knit fabric to avoid puckering.

When a length of yarn is finished, run it under several stitches on back of work

Fig. 10a   **Fig. 10b**

PICKING UP STITCHES

When instructed to pick up stitches, insert the needle from the **front** to the **back** under two strands at the edge of the worked piece (*Figs. 11a & b*). Put the yarn around the needle as if to **knit**, then bring the needle with the yarn back through the stitch to the right side, resulting in a stitch on the needle.
Repeat this along the edge, picking up the required number of stitches.
A crochet hook may be helpful to pull yarn through.

Fig. 11a   **Fig. 11b**

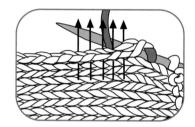   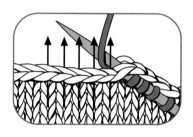

WEAVING SEAMS

With the **right** side of both pieces facing you and edges even, sew through both sides once to secure the seam. Insert the needle under the bar **between** the first and second stitches on the row and pull the yarn through (*Fig. 12*). Insert the needle under the next bar on the second side. Repeat from side to side, being careful to match rows. If the edges are different lengths, it may be necessary to insert the needle under two bars at one edge.

Fig. 12

FRINGE

Cut a piece of cardboard 6" (15 cm) wide and half as long as the required strands. Wind the yarn **loosely** and **evenly** lengthwise around the cardboard until the card is filled, then cut across one end; repeat as needed.

Hold together as many strands of yarn as specified in individual instructions; fold in half. With **wrong** side facing and using a crochet hook, draw the folded end up through a stitch and pull the loose ends through the folded end **(Fig. 13a)**; draw the knot up **tightly (Fig. 13b)**. Using photo as guide for placement, add fringe evenly spaced across.

Lay piece flat on a hard surface and trim the ends.

Fig. 13a

Fig. 13b

BASIC CROCHET STITCHES

YARN OVER (abbreviated YO)

Bring the yarn over the top of the hook from back to front, catching the yarn with the hook and turning the hook slightly toward you to keep the yarn from slipping off **(Fig. 14)**.

Fig. 14

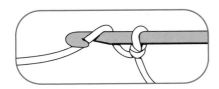

CHAIN (abbreviated ch)

YO, draw the yarn through the stitch on the hook **(Fig. 15)**.

Fig. 15

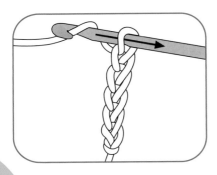

SINGLE CROCHET (abbreviated sc)

Insert hook in stitch indicated, YO and pull up a loop, YO and draw through both loops on hook **(Fig. 16)**.

Fig. 16

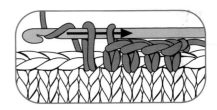

SLIP STITCH (abbreviated slip st)

Insert hook in stitch indicated, YO and draw through st and through loop on hook **(Fig. 17)**.

Fig. 17

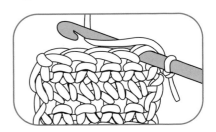